# South Cornwall: **Tea Shop** Walks

First published 2024 by:

**Northern Eye Books Limited**
Northern Eye Books, Tattenhall, Cheshire CH3 9PX
© Northern Eye Books Limited 2024

**ISBN 978-1-914589-19-5**

**Text:** *Vivienne Crow*

**Series editor:** *Tony Bowerman*

**Photographs:** *Vivienne Crow, 3idog.com, Adobe Stock, Dreamstime, Shutterstock, Alamy*

**Design:** *Carl Rogers and Laura Hodgkinson*

*Vivienne Crow has asserted her rights under the Copyright, Designs and Patents Act, 1988 to be identified as the author of this work. All rights reserved*

A CIP catalogue record for this book is available from the British Library.

*Printed in the UK on woodland-friendly FSC stock*

www.northerneyebooks.co.uk

 @northerneyebooks
@england_coast_path

 @northerneyeboo

 @northerneyebooks

For sales enquiries, please call 01928 723 744
Or email: tony@northerneyebooks.co.uk

**Important Advice:** The routes described in this book are undertaken at the reader's own risk. Walkers should take into account their level of fitness, wear suitable footwear and clothing, and carry food and water. It is also advisable to take the relevant OS map with you in case you get lost and leave the area covered by our maps.

Whilst every care has been taken to ensure the accuracy of the route directions, the publishers cannot accept responsibility for errors or omissions, or for changes in the details given. Nor can the publisher and copyright owners accept responsibility for any consequences arising from the use of this book.

If you find any inaccuracies in either the text or maps, please write or email us at the address above. Thank you.

*This book contains mapping data licensed from the Ordnance Survey with the permission of the Controller of Her Majesty's Stationery Office. © Crown copyright 2024 All rights reserved. License number 100047867*

**Cover:** *Kynance Cove Café, Lizard Peninsula (Walk 3)*

# Contents

South West Coast Path ............................. 4

Top 10 Walks: Tea Shop walks ................ 6

1 | Porthgwarra Cove Café, *Porthcurno* .... 8

2 | Mousehole Deli & Kitchen, *Mousehole* ..14

3 | Kynance Cove Café, *Lizard Peninsula*.. 20

4 | Croust House Kitchen, *Porthallow* .... 26

5 | Thirstea Company, *Portscatho* ............. 32

6 | Heligan Garden Kitchen, *Mevagissey* ..... 36

7 | Talland Bay Beach Café, *Looe* ................ 42

8 | Trevallick's Tea Room, *Bodmin Moor* .. 46

9 | The Orangery, *Mount Edgcumbe* ...... 52

10 | Lishe Coffee Shop, *Calstock* ............. 58

Useful Information ................................ 64

## South West Coast Path

RUNNING FOR 630 miles from Minehead in Somerset, around the tip of Land's End and back to South Haven Point at the mouth of Poole Harbour in Dorset, the South West Coast Path is one of Britain's longest National Trails. Bordered by the Bristol and English channels and looking out to the open Atlantic, it encompasses some of England's most spectacular and wildest coastline, where the diversity of plant, animal and insect life can be stunning. The seas, coves and surrounding hinterland has been a dramatic setting for a gloriously rich history, which have inspired countless tales of romance, drama and intrigue.

This series of **Top Ten Walks** explores highlights along the way; showcasing its natural beauty, wildlife and heritage and provoking imagination. Who knows, you may be inspired to come back to tackle the complete trail.

*Mullion Cove takes on purple hues at sunset*

## Tea Shops in South Cornwall

A walk on the South Cornwall coast without a visit to a tea shop is like Ant without Dec or fish without chips. What could be better than sitting down to afternoon tea—jam, first, of course!—at the end of a lovely walk along the crest of roller-coaster cliffs? Or tucking into a Cornish pasty while gazing out at a beautiful sandy bay? And you won't just find the time-honoured favourites; the cafés, tea shops and bistros of South Cornwall also serve up tasty brunches, vegan lunches and gluten-free cakes all washed down with excellent artisan coffees, local beers and even tea grown in the county. Modern or traditional, you'll find it here.

*"Tea would arrive, the cakes squatting on cushions of cream, toast in a melting shawl of butter, cups agleam…"*

Gerald Durrell

# TOP 10 Walks: Cafés, Tea Shops and Bistros

THE TEN TEA SHOPS, CAFÉS AND BISTROS here have been chosen partly because of the excellent walking that can be enjoyed from their doors and partly because of the fare and ambience they offer. They occupy beach, village, cliff-top and woodland locations. The walks themselves stretch almost the entire length of the coast—from Nanjizal, near Land's End to the Devon border. As well as spectacular cliff-tops, they take in beaches, bays, moorland, riversides and wildflower-filled woods as well as the fabulous viewpoints and heritage sites that help make Cornwall such a special place.

Porthgwarra Cove Café, Porthcurno — page 8

Mousehole Deli & Kitchen, Mousehole — page 14

Penrance Cove Café, Lizard Peninsula — page 20

Croust House Kitchen, Porthallow — page 26

Thirstea Company
Portscatho
page 32

Heligan Garden Kitchen
Mevagissey
page 36

Talland Bay Beach Café
Looe
page 42

Trevathan's Tea Room
Bodmin Moor
page 46

The Orangery
Mount Edgcumbe
page 52

Lishe.co
Calstock
page 58

*A sunny, sociable outdoor lunch at the Porthgwarra Cove Café*

# PORTHCURNO

# Porthgwarra Cove Café

*A hike in Cornwall's wild west, along rugged cliffs and across ancient farmland*

## walk 1

**What to expect:**
*Undulating cliffs with steep sections; good tracks; field paths*

**Distance/Time:** 9.5 kilometres/6 miles. Allow 2½-3 hours
**Start:** Main pay-and-display car park in Porthcurno (with PC)
**Grid ref:** SW 384 225
**Ordnance Survey Map:** Explorer 102, *Land's End*
**Café:** Porthgwarra Cove Café, Porthgwarra, near Penzance TR19 6JR | 01736 871754 | www.staubynestatescottages.co.uk

**Walk outline:** The area west of Porthcurno is home to some of the wildest and most enigmatic coastal scenery in Cornwall. Caves, chasms and secluded, sandy coves eat into high granite cliffs while the grassland on top is dotted with weird rock towers and prehistoric remains. Although it is a shame to leave the coast, the return route is almost as intriguing, crossing an agricultural landscape that's altered little since medieval times.

*About two kilometres from Porthcurno, the route drops into gorgeous Porthgwarra Cove, home to a tiny but idyllic beach and the Porthgwarra Cove Café. It may be a simple site, limited to outdoor seating only, but its location is hard to beat.*

*Tempting chalkboard*

### ▶ The Porthgwarra Cove Café at a glance

**Open:** Daily, 10am-3pm
**Food and specialities:** Light lunches, including some hot options such as chilli or soup; home-made cakes and pastries; and, most important of all for those hot summer days, Moomaid of Zennor ice-cream
**Beverages:** Tea, coffee, hot chocolate and soft drinks including smoothies
**Outside:** Outdoor seating only
**Dogs:** Dogs welcome

## The Walk

**1.** Take the broad path from the gate at the bottom end of the car park (near the public toilets). Ignore trails to the left and then the right. Nearing the **beach**, the path swings right. As other paths go left, keep right and then join a trail from the right. As you approach the rocks immediately below the **Minack Theatre**, the path heads very steeply up some stone steps. Entering a car park, follow the route marked on the ground for pedestrians and through a kissing-gate.

**2.** As you climb to the top of **Pedn-mên-an-mere**, ignore the faint trail to the left but then bear left at a fork immediately after this. The coast path dips and climbs, passing to the right of **St Levan's Well** as it does so. Dropping into **Porthgwarra**, keep left at two splits in the path. As you enter this charming hamlet, a rock tunnel on the left leads down to the tiny, **enclosed beach**. The main route though continues on the track and then goes left along a surfaced lane. (**Porthgwarra Cove Café** is on the right.)

**3.** As the lane bends right, climb the steps on the left to return to the cliffs. At the top of the rise, you're faced with the first of several choices. While the main path goes right, keeping back from the cliff edge, the more adventurous

© Crown copyright and/or database right. All rights reserved. Licence number 100047867

*Blue skies and crystal-clear water at Porthgwarra*

routes on the left pick their way across rugged ground where you can peer down on **zawns** (narrow, steep-sided chasms), fascinating rock formations and a **blowhole** created by the collapse of a sea cave. Offshore are stacks and islets where many boats have met their end over the centuries. While climbers test their mettle on the cliffs, divers explore the shipwrecks below. Choosing the left-hand route will also give you a better chance of spotting choughs, various seabirds and, in spring and early summer, colourful wildflower displays. Whichever path you take, you'll eventually pass to the left of the **lookout station** at **Gwennap Head**, built as a coastguard station in the early twentieth century and now manned by the volunteers of the National Coastwatch Institution who keep a visual watch on Britain's coasts.

**4.** After a dip and a rise, go through a gate and fork left, with the buildings at Land's End in view from time to time. Cross a small **stream** where the unusual moss- and lichen-covered rock towers of **Carn Trevean** loom over the path.

**5.** The next major drop on the coast path leads down to a path junction just above

*The cliff path winds above Porthgwarra's idyllic beach*

the tiny beach at **Nanjizal**. (There is a fenced mine opening here.) Reluctantly leaving this amazing section of coast, turn right. Go through the gate at the top of the rise and follow the track. Turn left at a T-junction and then go right at the next junction. Having swung left, between the buildings at **Higher Bosistow**, this old route winds its way across the farmland, enclosed by ancient walls covered in vegetation.

**6.** Go left at the road and, in just a few metres, turn right along the lane leading to **Raftra Farm**. Pass between the buildings and keep right at a fork. The track ends at a muddy area. Head left here and then go through the gate to the immediate right of the large farm shed.

**7.** Having walked 70 metres along the field edge, turn right through a gap in the crops. Continue in the same direction across a second field. After an awkward Cornish stile, go through the gate straight ahead. Always aiming for the church tower at St Levan, cross three more fields in the same direction (south-south-east). After the stile on the far side of the third of these, continue on a grassy trail. After another stile, walk with the field boundary on your right.

**8.** With the **church** on your right, turn sharp left at the next waymarker post.

Go through a gate and walk along the grass strip through the middle of the field, passing an **early Christian cross** along the way. From the buildings at **Rôspletha**, take the access track heading right. Reaching a surfaced lane, turn left and follow this down into **Porthcurno**. The car park is on the right at the bottom of the drop to complete the walk ♦

### St Levan's Well
*The water from this cliff-side spring is said to cure various ailments including toothache. Below the well are the remains of a chapel and cell used by St Levan, known locally as St Selevan, in the seventh century. He is said to have split in two a boulder linked with pagan fertility rites. Now known as the St Levan Stone, it is located in the grounds of the nearby parish church.*

*Exciting local produce at The Mousehole Deli and Kitchen*

## MOUSEHOLE

# Mousehole Deli & Kitchen

### walk 2

*Two contrasting perspectives on a lovely section of coast, starting from an idyllic fishing village*

**What to expect:**
*Village; coast path, rough and rocky in places; grassy fields; tracks*

**Distance/Time:** 8.5 kilometres/5½ miles. Allow 2¼-2¾ hours

**Start:** Pay-and-display car park on northern edge of Mousehole (height barrier)

**Grid ref:** SW 471 265

**Ordnance Survey Map:** Explorer 102, *Land's End*

**Café:** Mousehole Deli and Kitchen, North Cliffs, Mousehole TR19 6PH | 01736 732843 | www.mouseholedelikitchen.co.uk

**Walk outline:** This is a walk of two perfect halves. From the photogenic fishing village of Mousehole, the first half heads south along the coast path, across partly wooded, gently inclined cliffs before edging over steeper terrain. From tranquil Lamorna Cove, the route climbs and rewards walkers with further sea views, this time from the pretty farmland just above the cliffs. And, as if all that weren't enough, the Mousehole Deli and Kitchen means there's a treat at the end of the outing.

*Bored with sandwiches and paninis? The Mousehole Deli and Kitchen is the perfect antidote. Breakfast, lunch or dinner, you'll find something interesting on the menu of this harbourside restaurant.*

*On the coast path*

### ▶ Mousehole Deli and Kitchen at a glance

**Open:** Daily, 8am-9pm
**Food and specialities:** Menus change regularly depending on local availability, but include seafood, meat and vegan dishes. Examples include crab sandwiches, paella, soup and red mullet mini kebabs.
**Beverages:** The emphasis on local producers and suppliers continues with the hot drinks, soft drinks, wines, beers and spirits served; a range of non-alcoholic cocktails
**Outside:** None
**Dogs:** Special canine menu in downstairs restaurant

*A summer morning at Mousehole's sheltered harbour*

metres short of a cottage set apart from the main group, watch for a gate on the right. Cross the stile beside this and veer left. The path negotiates **two stiles and a bridge** over wet ground. Reaching an open area near **Kemyel Drea**, keep straight on and then turn left along the farm lane for 45 metres.

**5.** Now cross the stile on the right to walk the narrow passageway between **farm buildings**. In the next field, keep close to the building on the right and then cross a stile. (There is an old cross in the wall here.) Continue with the gorse-covered wall on your left, crossing five small fields. In the sixth field, gradually come away from the wall, aiming for the buildings at **Raginnis**.

**6.** Turn right at the road and then left along a gravel track. Keep straight on, eventually joining a grass path to the right of derelict **farm buildings**. Entering the field, you'll see two power poles to the left. Aim for the lower of these and pass through the gated gap in the field boundary. Still enjoying superb sea views, you can now see **Mousehole** ahead. Look for a gap in the wall ahead. Aim for a wooden post about 40 metres to the right of this. Cross a stile here. Maintain the same line (north-north-east) to cross another stile just above a metal farm gate. The steady descent continues on a faint, grassy trail.

Beyond a kissing-gate, drop to a **concrete track**. Turn left and quickly right along a signposted path. Keep straight on when this becomes surfaced, ignoring a turning on the right. The path later bends right, past villas on the left. Go left at a T-junction and then descend steps on the right. At the **harbour edge**, turn left to retrace your steps to the car park to complete the walk. ♦

### Pilchards

*Mousehole was once an important fishing harbour. It was exporting pilchards to France as early as the fourteenth century, with the industry reaching its peak in the eighteenth century. As in other Cornish villages, clifftop lookouts known as huers used to alert fishing teams to the location of shoals. Fishermen largely used seine nets at the time, with the catch later being pressed for its oil and then salted and packed into barrels.*

*Kynance Cove Cafe overlooks the popular beach*

# LIZARD PENINSULA

# Kynance Cove Café

## walk 3

*Heathland, cliffs and dramatic, rocky coves on the western side of the Lizard Peninsula*

**What to expect:**
*Heathland, muddy in places; cliffs; farmland*

**Distance/Time:** 13.5 kilometres/8½ miles. Allow 4½-5 hours

**Start:** Porthmellin car park on north-west side of B3296 (with honesty box)

**Grid ref:** SW 670 180

**Ordnance Survey Map:** Explorer 103, *The Lizard*

**Café:** Kynance Cove Café, Kynance Cove, Helston TR12 7PJ | 01326 290436 | www.kynancecovecafe.co.uk

**Walk outline:** The Lizard Peninsula is Britain's most southerly point with its own special character. Geology and climate work together here to allow an unusual range of wildflowers to thrive on the magnificent cliffs and heathland. Not surprisingly, the area is protected as a National Nature Reserve. As well as rare orchids, oxeye daisies and carpets of heather, you might also spot choughs, peregrines and seals on this relatively long walk from Mullion Cove. Head south across the heathland to Kynance Cove before returning along cliffs overlooking turquoise seas.

*Is this the most spectacularly located café in the UK? Probably. Roughly half-way into the walk, rest and refuel at one of the picnic tables while gazing down on rugged serpentine cliffs and sea stacks.*

*Spoilt for choice*

### ▶ Kynance Cove Cafe at a glance

**Open:** Daily, 9am-4pm (summer), 10am-3pm (winter); closed for part of December

**Food and specialities:** Simple café menu including sandwiches, salads, jacket spuds, hotdogs, burgers, pasties and homemade cakes and scones. Local suppliers where possible.

**Beverages:** Teas, hot chocolate and Fairtrade coffee; smoothies, milkshakes and other soft drinks; local beers and ciders

**Outside:** Mostly outdoor seating; only a few tables indoors

**Dogs:** Dogs on leads welcome

## The Walk

**1.** Turn right out of the **car park** and follow the road downhill. After 110 metres, turn left along a lane. This quickly swings left. Take the track rising to the right of the entrance of the **Mullion Cove Coastal Retreat**. As you near the top of the rise, there are two gates on the right. Cross the stile between them and follow the path, first along the field edge and then between stands of gorse. Cross three fields, keeping close to the boundary on the left all the while. (The second one has an old stone cross in it.) Reaching a road, maintain your line but on the asphalt now.

**2.** Just before the buildings at **Predannack Manor Farm**, take the track on the left. After this passes between gateposts near some cattle sheds, bear left along an enclosed path. Cross the stile at the far end and walk straight across the field. In a second field, keep close to the field boundary on your left and then turn right along a narrow lane. On reaching the buildings and National Trust parking area at **Higher Predannack Wollas**, turn left, soon following the track through a gate. Keep left beyond a small bridge, ignoring the trail to the coast on the right. About 40 metres after a gate, cross the stile on the right and continue

© Crown copyright and/or database right. All rights reserved. Licence number 100047867

Walk 3 – **Kynance Cove Café**, Lizard Peninsula ♦ 23

*Mullion Cove is a working harbour*

in the same direction as before along a **fenced trail**. (This area can be very muddy after heavy rain.)

**3.** A few metres beyond the next stile, at a junction of routes, cross the stile beside the gate on the right. A grassy route heads roughly south-south-east across this area of open access land. Having passed through a gate along the way, you will come to a solid track. Turn right along this and then, in a few metres, go left through a pedestrian gate. The route continues south-south-east, keeping close to the gorse on the right.

**4.** Turn left along a rough track near **Kynance Farm** and then keep left when another track heads right. The track later becomes less solid underfoot. When it ends, keep straight on until the ground ahead drops away steeply, with **Kynance Cove** directly below. Head right, to pass to the right of a rock outcrop. Stay on the grass and gradually swing down to the left but remember the cliff edge is just a few metres to your right here. On reaching a **National Trail** (white acorn) **waymarker**, veer left and drop into **Kynance Cove** with its perfectly placed

*White sand and emerald sea at Kynance Cove*

**café**. On a windy day, it can feel like there really is nowhere as wild as this, with white waves crashing up against the monstrous black rocks bearing names such as Lion Rock, Gull Rock and The Bishop.

**5.** From the cove, retrace your steps up to the National Trail waymarker and then up to the right. Where you came in earlier though, keep left, along the top of the cliffs. The climb is quickly over and you're able to stride out over grass-covered, flat-topped cliffs for the next 1.5 kilometres. It's only as the ground ahead suddenly plummets to **Soapy Cove** that the gentle walking is briefly interrupted.

**6.** Here, follow the trail inland a little way, ford the stream and then climb straight up the steep slope in front of you. This rough section of path soon ends and, at the top, you're met by another section of easy ambling on close-cropped grass. The path negotiates a couple of stiles and goes through a gate before dropping to cross a **stream** near **Lower Predannock**. The final 2.3 kilometres of cliff walking is over gently undulating ground with good views north-west across Mount's Bay to Cornwall's western tip. The stacks and islets of Mullion Cove appear, almost as dramatic as the scene at Kynance Cove.

**7.** You then find yourself standing directly above the village with the path descending steeply. At the bottom of the slope, turn right and then immediately left around the side of the house. Turn right along the road, and the **car park** where the walk began is on the left in about 300 metres. ♦

### Predannack Cross

*There are several hundred free-standing crosses in Cornwall, serving different purposes and featuring different designs. The one near Predannack Manor Farm (just before waypoint two) is a medieval, wheel-headed cross. Like many others in the county, this is a wayside cross and would've provided reassurance to travellers moving about the area. Although it was re-erected in the nineteenth century, it remains in its original location.*

*Croust House Kitchen is a Cornish delight*

# PORTHALLOW

# Croust House Kitchen

## walk 4

*Lovely, meandering ramble across rolling countryside with great views of the coast*

**What to expect:** *Country lanes; field paths; quiet coves; secluded hamlets*

**Distance/Time:** 8.5 kilometres/5½ miles. Allow 2¼-2¾ hours

**Start:** Beachside car park at Porthallow

**Grid ref:** SW 797 231

**Ordnance Survey Map:** Explorer 103, *The Lizard*

**Café:** Croust House Kitchen at Roskilly's, Tregellast Barton Farm, St Keverne TR12 6NX | 01326 280479 | www.roskillys.co.uk

**Walk outline:** With beautiful views that change with every twist and turn, this walk explores the rolling countryside on the eastern side of the Lizard peninsula. Setting off from Porthallow, the walk heads inland. It calls in at tiny hamlets and the village of St Keverne before passing the café at Roskilly's open farm and then dropping to the tiny bay at Porthoustock. The walk ends on an inland section of the coast path.

*It's always a treat to visit the welcoming Croust House Kitchen, whether it's for a vegan breakfast, an imaginative lunch or just a home-made ice-cream. About half-way through the walk, the café has a spacious indoor dining area as well as a pretty courtyard.*

Proper coffee

### ▶ Croust House Kitchen at a glance

**Open:** Tues-Sat, 10am-8pm; Sun and Mon, 10am-6pm
**Food and specialities:** Range of breakfast and brunch options; hearty home-made dishes, burgers and wood-fired pizzas with unusual toppings; home-made ice-cream; children's menu
**Beverages:** Hot drinks; smoothies and milkshakes; local beers, ciders and soft drinks; wine by the bottle or glass
**Outside:** Large courtyard with several tables, some partially under cover
**Dogs:** Dogs in courtyard only

*Fishing boats drawn up onto the shingle at Porthallow*

## The Walk

**1.** Leave the **car park** and turn right along the road. When the lane bends right to begin climbing, keep straight ahead – along a lane passing to the left of some cottages. Follow the lane to the left and then turn right along a gravel track in front of **Respryn House**. The route ahead narrows as it passes to the right of the last cottage. At the end of this fenced section, climb the short slope on the left and then swing right—up some steps. Emerging in a field, keep straight ahead (west). Cross a grass track diagonally right to enter another field. Continue steadily uphill with the hedgerow on your left. When this boundary bends left, strike off south-west (or keep to the field edge if there are crops in it). Exiting the field via a stile in the hedge, ignore the road on the right; simply keep straight ahead along the lane heading for **Tregarne**.

**2.** After entering the hamlet, take the first track on the left. This enters and crosses a field. On the far side, keep straight on—along a more enclosed track—for just a few strides and then enter the field on your left. Without waymarkers or a path on the ground, walk south-east to a narrow gap in the hedge on the far side. After a wooden stile, descend steeply with a hedgerow on your left. At the bottom, locate a stile hidden behind the high vegetation on the left. Beyond this, a trail winds its way down to the road near **Tregarne Mill**. Turn right.

**3.** At a T-junction, climb the steps on the opposite side of the road. Head straight up the field (south-south-west). On the far side, continue uphill with the field boundary on your right. Keep close to this hedgerow across two more fields. At the far end of the second of these, a more obvious trail develops, dropping into a pretty, wooded valley. Cross the track and the little stream to join a clear path heading uphill. This becomes a surfaced lane on the edge of **St Keverne**. Go left at the road and follow it to the right, passing around the side of the **village square** and in front of the **White Hart pub**.

**4.** Go straight over at the crossroads – along **Trelyn Road**. When the lane swings right, cross the steps next

*Working boats at Porthoustock cove*

to the metal gate to the left of the bend —effectively straight on. Keep close to the fence on your left across two fields. In the third one, come away from the field boundary slightly, aiming for a narrow gap on the far side. Turn left along the road and you'll pass the entrance to **Roskilly's Croust House Kitchen** on the right in 180 metres.

**5.** At a staggered junction, cross diagonally left to join a narrow lane. Go right at a T-junction. About 210m beyond the **hamlet of Rosenithon**, the road bends right. Just after it does so, cross a stile in the hedgerow on your left (near a gate) and cross the field diagonally right (north-east). Beyond a gap in the hedges, follow the same line across two more fields, rejoining the road just above a white-washed cottage. Head downhill and turn right at a T-junction—towards **Porthoustock**.

**6.** From the **cove**, follow the road uphill for about 120 metres. When it swings right, keep straight on—following the coast path along a track passing to the left of a house. After the last cottage, step up to the right and then bear right through a kissing-gate. The trail follows a fence steeply uphill. When the fence bears left, keep straight ahead, through a kissing-gate. Go right in the next field and then left to exit via a gap in the fence. Continue in the same direction on the asphalt. Follow the road round to the right in tiny **Trenance**.

**7.** When the road later bends left, cross the lane coming in from the right to join a shady path that starts just to the left of a metal gate. Turn left along a track at the bottom of some steps and then keep right at a fork to go through a gate. Turn right at the road to drop back into **Porthallow** to complete the walk. ♦

### Quarrying

*The large concrete silo at Porthoustock once stored stone from the nearby quarry ready for loading on to ships. It is now disused, but aggregate continues to be quarried and is loaded direct to ships from the pier on the south side of the little bay. The green-tinged diorite found here is used as building aggregate and, during World War Two, helped construct some of Cornwall's many military airfields.*

*Enjoy tasty food and local produce at the Thirstea Company*

# PORTSCATHO

# walk 5

# Thirstea Company

*An easy stretch of coastal walking on the tranquil Roseland Peninsula*

**What to expect:** *Gentle coast path; village; farm lane*

**Distance/Time:** 8 kilometres/5 miles. Allow 2-2¼ hours

**Start:** Portscatho and Porthcurnick Beach car park on northern edge of Portscatho

**Grid ref:** SW 876 357

**Ordnance Survey Map:** Explorer 105, *Falmouth & Mevagissey*

**Café:** The Thirstea Company, Porth Farm, St Anthony, Portscatho TR2 5EX | 01872 580773 | www.thethirsteacompany.co.uk

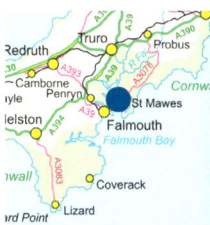

**Walk outline:** Starting from near the peaceful fishing village of Portscatho, this is about as gentle as coastal walking gets in rugged Cornwall. The route heads south along the edge of fields and above rocky outcrops. From Towan Beach, it heads inland, returning along wildflower-fringed tracks and lanes that run parallel with the outward, coastal route. Minimal ascent along the way means you're in for an easy stroll with the added benefit of a super little café at the half-way mark.

*The Thirstea Company above Towan Beach makes for a great spot to break this lovely amble. Seth and Jodi serve up simple but tasty food, made with good-quality produce that is "grown, made, roasted, reared, laid or churned in Cornwall".*

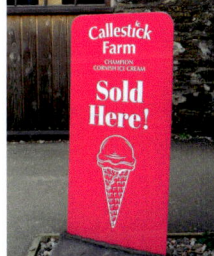

*Cornish ice cream*

### ▶ The Thirstea Company at a glance

**Open:** Summer, daily 10am-5pm; winter, 10am-4pm, closed Fridays
**Food and specialities:** Hearty soups, sandwiches, toasties and pasties. A variety of cakes and traybakes. Ice-cream from Callestick Farm, based near Truro
**Beverages:** Teas and coffee from local suppliers; Cornish-made soft drinks
**Outside:** Several picnic tables
**Dogs:** Well-behaved dogs welcome

## The Walk

**1.** Turn right out of the car park and, in less than 100 metres, turn right along an easy-to-miss shady path with a sign indicating it is "unsuitable for motor vehicles". At the top of the steps dropping to **Porthcurnick beach**, climb the steps on the right to join the coast path heading south. Having ignored a few trails leading back up to the car park, join a surfaced lane. Go straight over a crossing of lanes in **Portscatho** and then turn left at the T-junction, walking above the bay.

*Portscatho is a tranquil spot, some way from the usual Cornish tourist haunts. This small bay was once a centre for pilchard fishing. Today, it is home to a few small galleries and other businesses.*

**2.** At the end of the lane, bend right to continue on the **coast path**. This is about as easy as coastal walking gets—the path is mostly level, it's in good condition and an added bonus is that walkers get to look down on the seabirds resting on the rock outcrops directly below. Eventually, having passed around **Greeb Point** and 2.5 kilometres after leaving Portscatho, you go through a gate and pass a **National Trust sign** announcing you've arrived at **Towan Beach**.

**3.** There is a crossing of paths at the southern end of the beach. You can access the sand by heading left, but the main route goes right here —signposted Porth. A path on the left peels off to pay a visit to the **Thirstea Company café**. Alternatively, to continue on the walk, keep to the main path until you reach the road. Turn right and, in 30 metres, fork right along the hedge-lined

© Crown copyright and/or database right. All rights reserved. Licence number 100047867

Curving sands at Porthcurnick beach

track climbing steadily. When the track bends left, keep straight ahead on grass —over a stile and through a gate. Join a partly sealed lane.

**4.** Turn right at the road in **Gerrans**, soon enjoying good views out to sea. Opposite the **memorial hall car park**, head left up **Stodden Steps**. The path goes left, then right and up into a cul-de-sac (California Gardens). Follow the road down to the right and then turn left along **Treventon Road**. Go right at the T-junction and, in just a few strides, take the signposted footpath on the left beside a bungalow called Seacroft. After a gate, bear half-right across the field. Cross the main road to re-enter the car park where the walk started to complete the walk. ♦

### Shipwreck

*In December 1961, the British Cadet-class tanker SS Allegrity struck Greeb Point while en route from Le Havre to the Stanlow oil refinery at Ellesmere Port. She was refloated but later capsized further along the Roseland Peninsula, spilling 800 tonnes of crude oil into the sea and on to local beaches. Despite gale-force winds and rough seas, her 14-strong crew were saved by the volunteers of the Falmouth Lifeboat.*

*Families are always welcome at the Heligan Garden Kitchen*

# MEVAGISSEY/LOST GARDENS OF HELIGAN

## walk 6

# Heligan Garden Kitchen

*Cliff paths, rolling farmland and a visit to an iconic visitor attraction*

**Distance/Time:** 9 kilometres/5½ miles. Allow 2¾-3¼ hours

**Start:** Willow car park on B3273 in Mevagissey

**Grid ref:** SX 012 450

**Ordnance Survey Map:** Explorer 105, *Falmouth & Mevagissey*

**Café:** The Heligan Garden Kitchen, Pentewan, St Austell, PL26 6EN | 01726 845100 | www.heligan.com

**What to expect:**
*Undulating coast path; fields; shared-use cycle path;*

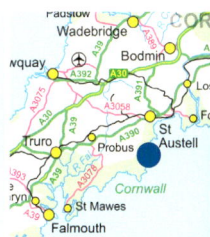

**Walk outline:** This walk starts from the bustling village of Mevagissey where shops, galleries and cafés line the narrow streets, and fishing boats still come and go from the picturesque harbour. It follows the coast path north for a short while before heading inland across rolling farmland and in and out of pretty woodland to reach the famous Lost Gardens of Heligan. Take a break for lunch or treat yourself to afternoon tea here before a gentle stroll back to Mevagissey.

*The Heligan Garden Kitchen is an understandably popular restaurant, serving up good-quality, home-made food as part of the Lost Gardens of Heligan complex. Some of the fruit and vegetables are grown in the surrounding gardens.*

*Tempting sandwiches*

### ▶ Heligan Garden Kitchen at a glance

**Open:** Daily, 9am-6pm (summer), 10am-4pm (winter)
**Food and specialities:** Cooked breakfast until 11.30am; soups, salads and other wholesome dishes, some featuring ingredients from the gardens. Children's menu. Many gluten-free and vegetarian options. Massive cake display.
**Beverages:** Teas, coffee and soft drinks; wines, including Prosecco, by the bottle or glass
**Outside:** Outside tables for takeaway options
**Dogs:** Well-behaved dogs welcome

## The Walk

**1.** Leave the **car park** and turn left along the road. As the traffic heads left along the one-way system, keep straight ahead, soon passing the **River Street short-stay car park** on your left. Follow the road round a tight bend to the left and then take the next narrow lane on the left (Church Street). Almost immediately, bear right along the cobbles of **St George's Square**. The cobbles end when you emerge on the **harbourside**. Keep straight ahead, along **East Wharf**, walking with the water on your right. Nearing **Mevagissey Museum** at the far end of East Wharf, you'll see a wall on your left. The coast path heads uphill on the other side of this wall. It's very easy to miss the start of this path but, once you're on it, you should follow it to the top and then turn right. Ignore the path to the left at the top of the first set of steps; simply keep climbing. Emerging at an open area, keep close to the bushes on the right and follow them up to the end of a **row of terraced houses**. Here

*Working boats line the busy harbour at Mevagissey*

you join a surfaced path along the cliff top and above the beach at **Polstreath**.

**2.** The path dips, crosses a **footbridge** and climbs steeply out the other side on steps. After the kissing-gate at the top, keep close to the gorse on the right, still heading uphill for now. You then negotiate a series of gates and stiles before the path drops to **Portgiskey**.

**3.** After crossing the long **bridge** at the bottom of the drop, veer right to climb again. Go through a gate to reach a path T-junction. Turn right here, walking parallel with the **B3273**. Cross the lane leading into the **Pentewan Sands Holiday Park** and continue along the pavement beside the main road.

**4.** About 90 metres after passing the road turning on the right for Pentewan, take the signposted track rising to the left of the road. This winds its way uphill and peters out at a gate. Beyond this, continue uphill through two fields with the field boundary on your left. The path goes straight through the middle of three more fields, continuing in the same direction. When you reach a hedgerow preventing further progress in this

*The exciting suspension bridge at Heligan*

direction, bear left along a track. About 70 metres into the next field, cross a stile in the wall on the right. Veer left along a trail through the woods. When this drops on to a **surfaced cycle track**, turn left.

**5.** Soon after passing under the road, keep straight ahead at a path junction—signposted Heligan Gardens. Reaching a **campsite**, keep straight on, passing the reception and shop on your right. Keep to this track through the site until it passes to the left of a small lodge partly concealed by trees. Just after this, go through the gate over to the right. Cross a driveway and go through the gate opposite to enter the car park of the **Lost Gardens of Heligan**. The gardens, rediscovered in 1990, are open daily to the public. There is an admission fee, but you don't have to pay if you just want to visit the restaurant.

**6.** Go right and immediately left, as if heading for the overflow car park, but then turn left along a broad track. To visit the **Heligan Garden Kitchen**, go left at the entrance to the gardens in a short while and turn right just before the **toilet blocks**. (The entrance to the restaurant is on the left in a few metres.) Alternatively, to continue on the walk, keep to the main track. When it begins descending, bear left at a fork.

**7.** Pass between the buildings at **Heligan Mill**. This idyllic property started life as a water-powered corn mill and, with the help of crowdfunding, the current tenants are reinstating the old orchard, walled hop yard and paddocks. Bear right after the **tiny bridge**. You later join a surfaced cycle route coming down from the left. Follow this to the **B3273** and turn right. The car park where the walk started is on the left in about 350 metres. ♦

### Lost Gardens of Heligan

*The gardens surrounding Heligan House were nearly lost forever when the workforce who tended the site went off to fight in World War One, many never to return. It was only in 1990 that the derelict gardens were rediscovered among the brambles, and Europe's largest restoration project of its type began. Today, the 200-acre site is open to the public and includes productive plots, decorative gardens where exotic species thrive and the 'Jungle'.*

*The stylish Talland Bay Beach Cafe*

# LOOE

# Talland Bay Beach Café

*A hike along cliffs to a beautiful bay, returning via woods where a giant once roamed*

**Distance/Time:** 12 kilometres/7.5 miles. Allow 3½-4 hours

**Start:** Millpool pay-and-display riverside car park in West Looe (with PC)

**Grid ref:** SX 250 537

**Ordnance Survey Map:** Explorer 107, *St Austell & Liskeard*

**Café:** Talland Bay Beach Café, Talland Bay, Looe PL13 2JA | 01503 272088 | www.tallandbaybeachcafe.co.uk

## walk 7

**What to expect:**
*Town; cliffs; country tracks and lanes; woodland*

**Walk outline:** Looe sits at the mouth of the River Looe, the waterway that splits this small fishing town in two. Buildings cling to the steep valley sides in both West Looe and the busier East Looe, creating a photogenic scene. This walk sets out from the town along a lovely clifftop path as far as Talland Bay. Heading inland on old tracks and quiet country lanes with far-reaching views, it then enters the valley of the West Looe River to meander back under a dense woodland canopy.

*The family-run Talland Bay Café occupies an enviable location in one of south Cornwall's prettiest coves. Take a break from your walk here, about half-way into the route, and watch the waves wash over the rocks and tiny beach while you refuel.*

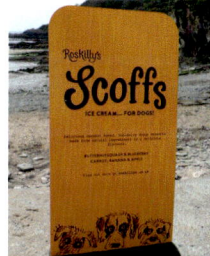

*Doggy delights!*

### ▶ Talland Bay Beach Café at a glance

**Open:** End of March to end of Oct only; daily, 9.30am-4.30pm
**Food and specialities:** Soup, pasties, paninis and sandwiches, including local crab. Children's menu. Homemade traybakes, cakes and cream teas. Roskilly's award-winning ice-creams
**Beverages:** Hot drinks including locally roasted Origin coffee; soft drinks; wine, lager and Cornish beers and ciders
**Outside:** Mostly outdoor seating, including some tables under cover
**Dogs:** Welcome, and there's even doggy ice-cream available

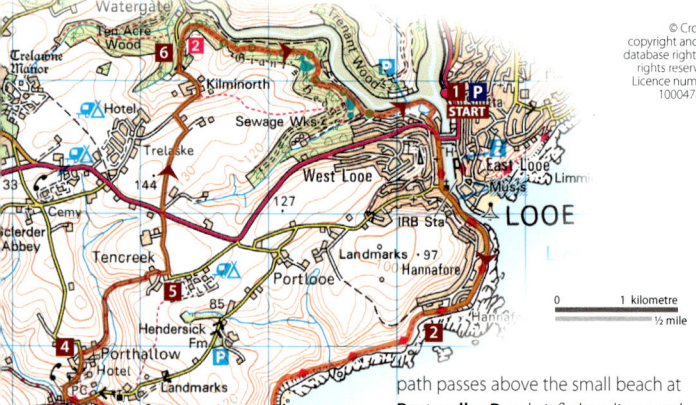

## The Walk

**1.** Make your way to the **river** and turn right along the path. On reaching metal railings, head away from the river. Go left along the lane beside **Looe Chandlery** to reach the **A387**. Turn left and immediately go right along **Quay Road**. Keeping the water on your left—first the river, then the sea—walk this road until it ends near **Hannafore Point**.

**2.** Go through the gate and keep to the lower path. *Looe Island is just off shore, the site of Lammana Priory before it moved to the mainland in medieval times.* The first significant climb begins as you reach National Trust land at **Hendersick**. The path passes above the small beach at **Portnadler Bay**, briefly heading south before it swings west again. You'll soon see **Talland Bay** ahead, a small, mostly rocky cove with a few perfectly located houses perched above it among the trees. Later, with the bay directly below, make sure you head sharp left with the well-worn path. Beyond the gate at the bottom of the steps, cross the small parking area and turn left along the lane.

**3.** To visit the **cove and café**, take the next turning on the left. Alternatively, to continue on the main route, keep straight on, soon climbing a narrow stretch of lane.

**4.** About 370 metres beyond the turning for the café, turn right along **Porthallow Farm**'s access lane. This later narrows and drops steadily into a steep-sided valley. Cross the **stream** in the bottom and climb the track on the other side.

*The rugged coast at Talland Bay*

**5.** Turn left at a T-junction near the cottages at **Tencreek**. Carefully cross the **A387**, continuing on a quiet lane. A double-gate near the top of the rise provides a great view up the wooded gorge of the West Looe River, stretching far to the north. Soon after this, the road bends left to descend into the valley.

**6.** Almost 1.5 kilometres after crossing the A387, bear right along a broad path leading up to the gate into **Kilminorth Wood**. As narrower trails lead left and right, keep to this path until it joins a riverside path from the left. After the gate, descend the lane and then keep left beside the **West Looe River**, fishing ground for egrets. The car park where the walk started is on your right. ♦

### Beware of giants!
*Soon after entering Kilminorth Wood, you'll see a stone-faced earth bank beside the path. This is known as the Giant's Hedge and is thought to date from the sixth century. Once almost 15 kilometres long and flanked by a ditch, it is thought to have been a defensive structure. The only sign of giants though are the massive beech trees growing out of the top of it.*

*Good-looking ploughmans*

# BODMIN MOOR

## walk 8

## Trevallick's Farm Shop & Tea Room

*A moorland meander that takes in a prehistoric enigma and photogenic mining ruins*

**What to expect:** *Moorland tracks and trails; road; disused tramways*

**Distance/Time:** 11.5 kilometres/7¼ miles. Allow 3-3½ hours

**Start:** Hurlers car park on south-west edge of Minions

**Grid ref:** SX 259 711

**Ordnance Survey Map:** Explorer 109, *Bodmin Moor*

**Café:** Trevallick's Farm Shop and Tea Room, Pensilva, Liskeard PL14 5PJ | 01579 364061 | www.trevallicks.com

**Walk outline:** The moorland around the tiny settlement of Minions is not only picturesque, it's fascinating. This walk passes a mysterious line of stone circles dating from prehistoric times as well as reminders of the area's mining heritage, with engine houses, chimneys and shafts. Hawthorn, oak and gorse line the routes of disused tramways while old tracks head out over the open grassland—making light work of navigation on this south-eastern edge of Bodmin Moor.

*The fact that Trevallick's attracts locals as well as visitors speaks volumes. This friendly café serves up tasty food from a lovely spot high on a moorland road. Sit outside for great views of Dartmoor in the hazy blue distance.*

*Summer tables*

### ▶ Trevallick's Farm Shop & Tea Room at a glance

**Open:** Mon-Sat, 9am-4pm, Sun 10am-3pm
**Food and specialities:** Breakfasts, big and small; sandwiches, jacket spuds (with children's options), pasties, ploughman's lunches; afternoon teas including a special 'gin-tasting' option with four artisan gins
**Beverages:** Hot drinks including Cornwall-grown Tregothnan tea; soft drinks; wine, gins, beers and ciders
**Outside:** Several tables including some 'pods'
**Dogs:** Welcome outside and in conservatory

## The Walk

**1.** Climb the few steps at the end of the car park furthest from the road, swing left across the grass and then turn right along a track heading out across open moorland. Before long, you'll see **The Hurlers stone circles** to the right. This is access land, so you can wander over to have a closer look if you want. Otherwise, continue on the track.

**2.** Bear right when the route eventually splits in three. Pass through an area of **fenced mine workings** and then climb to the south of the granite tors perched atop **Stowe's Hill**. At the crest of the rise, you can see the monument on Kit Hill to the east. Beyond that is Dartmoor. At a fork, keep right along a grassy route that's easier underfoot. It later rejoins the stony track which is followed past a locked gate and beside a car park.

**3.** On reaching a road junction, ignore the first lane on the left; instead turn left along the road signed to Upton Cross and Rilla Mill. After a cattle grid,

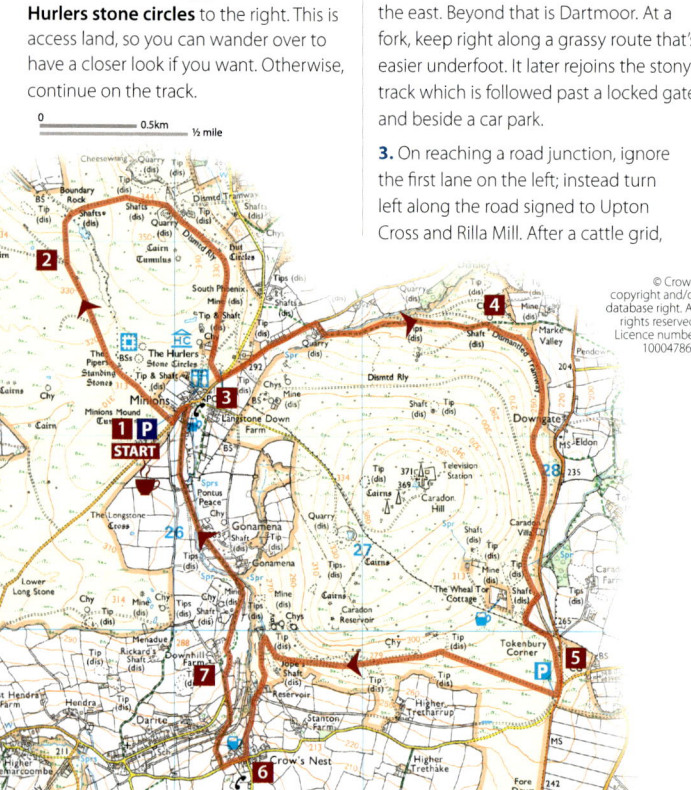

© Crown copyright and/or database right. All rights reserved. Licence number 100047867

*Heading through an archway below the ruined engine house*

pass some houses on the left and then a small cottage hidden in a hollow to the right. Immediately after the latter, go through the pedestrian gate on the right to access a fenced path. Beyond the gate at the bottom of this, ford the **small stream** and turn left along a trail beside the water. This later comes away from the stream slightly, guided by **waymarker posts**. The route is lined by gorse and hawthorn. As it drops into an oak-filled dell, bear right at a fork.

4. Soon after joining a stony path from the right, you emerge from the gorse to see two trails swinging right. Take the one further right. This contours the eastern base of **Caradon Hill**, following the route of a disused tramway along the edge of sparse oak woodland. Keep left as this later joins a broader path and then a rough vehicle track, which leads to a road.

5. To visit **Trevallick's Farm Shop and Tea Room**, turn left and walk along the road for about 120 metres. Otherwise, take the track on the right just before the road. When this reaches the edge of a rough parking area, turn right along another track, quickly passing between two metal barriers. Keep to the clearest

*Granite tors on Stowe's Hill near Minions, Bodmin Moor*

track past some spoil heaps. Nearing a group of **mine buildings**, you'll see a tracking joining from the left. Soon after this, turn left to walk through an archway beside an **engine house**. Keep straight on, soon picking up the line of two parallel tracks. Take the lower one. It swings right, making its way past **chimneys and engine houses**, and then bends left. *Most of the disused workings that can be seen in this area today date from the nineteenth century when Caradon Hill was mined extensively for copper and tin. The tall buildings are engine houses.* Follow the track under an old railway and out to a road.

**6.** Turn right, past the **Crows' Nest pub** and then take the rough track on the right. The bridleway climbs, later becoming a surfaced lane. At the next junction, keep right.

**7.** Go through the gate to the right of **Downhill Barn**'s driveway. Keep close to the fence on your left until it bends left. Now continue straight ahead on the track. When this bends left near some spoil heaps, keep straight on, descending a narrower trail. This swings left and enters a cutting. You're now following the route of the old Liskeard and Caradon Railway built in 1844 to serve the mines. Pass through two gates and continue up the old railway, its surface lined by slabs of stone. After briefly emerging from the cutting, cross a grass track to rejoin the old routeway. Maintaining your line, join a track near a cottage, through a gate and to the left of a fenced compound. Beyond a small gate, the tramway's route is more obvious again as it continues between low walls. Join a rough track on the edge of **Minions**. Turn left at the road. The car park where the walk started is on the right in 100 metres. ♦

### The Hurlers

*The moorland in this area is dotted with prehistoric remains including The Hurlers. This trio of stone circles is arranged in a line, a grouping found nowhere else in England. They date from the late Neolithic or early Bronze Age, and, according to local mythology, are the remains of men who were turned to stone for playing hurling on the Sabbath. The two standing stones to the west of the circles are known as The Pipers.*

*Upmarket fare in the stylish Orangery*

# MOUNT EDGCUMBE AND KINGSAND

# The Orangery

*Rivers, woods and coast on a circuit of a peninsula jutting out into Plymouth Sound*

**Distance/Time:** 10.5 kilometres/6½ miles. Allow 2½-3 hours

**Start:** Cremyll pay-and-display car park

**Grid ref:** SX 452 532

**Ordnance Survey Map:** Explorer 108, *Lower Tamar Valley & Plymouth*

**Café:** The Orangery, Mount Edgcumbe Park, Torpoint PL10 1HZ | 01752 822586 | www.theorangerymountedgcumbe.co.uk

## walk 9

**What to expect:**
*Woodland; fields; country park; riverside*

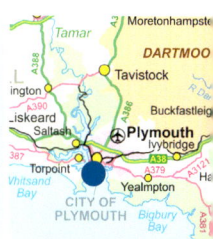

**Walk outline:** This walk explores one arm of the peninsula reaching out into Plymouth Sound at the south-eastern corner of Cornwall. From Cremyll, where a boat has been ferrying travellers across the River Tamar for more than 1,000 years, the route winds through riverside woodland, across farmland and down into the pretty seaside village of Kingsand. Here it picks up the South West Coast Path which it follows in and out of bluebell woods and through Mount Edgcumbe Country Park.

*Built in the eighteenth century in Mount Edgcumbe's Italian Garden, the Orangery is located just a few hundred metres from the end of the walk. Indulge in a full breakfast, tuck into a hearty lunch or spoil yourself with a decadent afternoon tea.*

*Orangery counter*

### ▶ The Orangery at a glance

**Open:** Daily, 10.30am-3pm
**Food and specialities:** Breakfast and brunch from 10.30am; sandwiches; lunchtime menu includes salads, burgers, tarts; children's menu; Sunday roast from noon to 3pm
**Beverages:** Organic Fairtrade teas and coffees; locally made, organic soft drinks; Fever Tree tonics; wide range of alcoholic drinks, including beers, wines, spirits and liqueurs
**Outside:** Outdoor tables beside the Italianate water fountain
**Dogs:** Well-behaved dogs welcome

## The Walk

**1.** Leave the **car park** and turn left along the road. Drawing level with a **water fountain** on the right, and just before the **Edgcumbe Arms**, take the track on the left. Bear left at a fork and then, about 200 metres beyond the road, take the path signposted to the right. You're soon walking with the river directly below, heading up a tributary arm of the **Tamar** known as **Millbrook Lake**. On reaching **Empacombe**, keep straight ahead – down a surfaced lane and out to a grassy area beside a small harbour. Turn left and walk around the harbour edge, re-entering the trees beyond the buildings. The path skirts the bottom edge of fields, swinging left to reach a road at a stile.

**2.** Cross over and go through the kissing-gate opposite. Follow the track for about 50 metres and then head up a grassy path on the right. Just before the trees, turn round for a good view back up the Tamar beyond Torpoint. At a fork, keep left on a path between the brambles. After a kissing-gate, turn right. Where a less well walked path keeps straight on, turn sharp left. The path then swings steeply up to the right, a rope line acting as a guide. Cross a woodland track, up the steps opposite and continue to a road.

Walk 9 – **The Orangery,** Mount Edgcumbe & Kingsand ♦ 55

*The atmospheric coastal settlement at Kingsand*

**3.** Cross the road and follow the trail opposite to a small gate. Once through this, head towards **Maker Church**. At a lane junction, go straight across, walking to the right of the church. Drawing level with its gate, turn right, walking beside the hedgerow on the left. Immediately after a farm gate, cross the stile on the left. Walk with the hedgerow on your left through this field and then follow the beaten earth trail left and then right. This enclosed path leads down to a concrete track next to a detached house. Go straight over and follow the path through the next field. Veer slightly right in a second field.

**4.** Turn right at the road and go left at the T-junction near **Maker Farm**. Beyond **Hawkins Battery**, the views across Plymouth Sound open out. Take the next path on the left, descending towards **Kingsand Beach**. Bear right at a clear fork. After passing an old **coastal battery** covered by vegetation, the path begins a steady descent. Bear left at the next fork, dropping more steeply. Follow a surfaced path into **Kingsand**. This quickly broadens to become a lane.

*Fort Picklecombe at Torpoint is now a hotel*

**5.** After about 40 metres on this lane, take the coast path signposted to the left and through the gate. (Or continue downhill between wonky cottages to explore the village.) Turn right on reaching a lane above **Hooe Lake Point** and, after about 50 metres, go through the gate on the left. Keep to the path just above the road for now. After entering woodland, bear left at a fork, still following the coast path's acorn symbols.

**6.** Soon after passing above **Fort Picklecombe**, you reach a **barrier** across the path. Take the narrower path climbing left. This zig-zags uphill. Following coast path waymarkers; don't be tempted by a trail straight on at a sharp right bend. Ignore some steps down and then fork left, up some **stone steps**. Pass to the right of a small **stone shelter** and then go through a gate to descend through bluebell woods. At the bottom of a flight of **steps**, cross a track and continue down **more steps**.

**7.** About 300 metres beyond a solitary house in the woods, take the coast path signed to the right of the track, soon passing through a tall gate to re-enter the woods. Before long, you drop to sea level again and are looking straight across the water to Devon. Join a surfaced path heading in your direction and keep

Walk 9 – **The Orangery,** Mount Edgcumbe & Kingsand ♦ 57

straight on at a junction near some picnic benches. Entering **Mount Edgcumbe**'s **historic gardens**, keep to the right of the **blockhouse** and then pass to the left of **The Orangery**. Soon after going through an **archway**, turn right to exit the country park. Take the next path on your left and then go left at the road. The **Cremyll car park** is on your right in 120 metres. ♦

### Mount Edgcumbe

*Mount Edgcumbe House, the former home of the Earls of Mount Edgcumbe, was built in the mid-sixteenth century. The Grade II listed building, restored after being destroyed by German bombers in World War Two, is set in a Grade I listed landscape covering 865 acres. The seventh earl sold the estate to Cornwall County Council and Plymouth City Council in 1971 and it has been open as a country park since 1988.*

*Superb coffee at the Lishe Coffee Shop*

## CALSTOCK AND COTEHELE

# walk 10

# Lishe Coffee Shop

*An exploration of the delightful Tamar Valley, its woods and historic buildings*

**What to expect:**
*Quiet lanes; woodland; riverside paths*

**Distance/Time:** 9 kilometres/5½miles. Allow 3-3½ hours

**Start:** Riverside car park (with PC) at eastern end of Calstock, behind village hall

**Grid ref:** SX 436 684

**Ordnance Survey Map:** Explorer 108, *Lower Tamar Valley & Plymouth*

**Café:** Lishe Coffee Shop, 6 Commercial Road, Calstock PL18 9QT | 01822 832323

**Walk outline:** Calstock occupies a pretty location on a meandering, tidal section the River Tamar. The walk heads downstream from the village, passing through the dense broadleaf woods that cover the steep valley sides. There's no shortage of historic interest along the way, with the route calling in at the National Trust's Cotehele Quay, picturesque Cotehele Mill and Cotehele House, a fascinating Tudor home with beautiful gardens.

*Small but perfectly formed — that's the Lishe Coffee Shop. This is a great place, either before you set off or when you finish the walk, to just sit over a cup of coffee and watch the world go by.*

*Special coffees*

### ▶ The Lishe Coffee Shop at a glance

**Open:** Wed-Sun, 9.45am-4pm
**Food and specialities:** Simple menu – rolls, including some hot fillings until 2pm; cakes and traybakes
**Beverages:** Wide range of teas and coffees from local supplier; soft drinks
**Outside:** A few tables outside
**Dogs:** Warmly welcomed with treats

## The Walk

**1.** From the car park, head to the left of the **village hall** to join a **wooden walkway**. When this ends, keep close to the **River Tamar** until you can go no further along its banks. Now swing up the lane to the right, just past the **Tamar Inn**. Then, with the **Lishe Coffee Shop** opposite, go left at the junction. There are two turnings on the left in quick succession. Take the second of these, known as **Lower Kelly**. This passes under **Calstock Viaduct**, which carries the Tamar Valley Line over the river, and then past **Calstock Boatyard**. Nearing the end of the lane, keep left at a fork.

**2.** Just after a **row of cottages**, take the path signed to Cotehele House on the left, soon climbing through the woods. *Glimpses of the river and the viaduct come and go between the trees. Built from concrete blocks in the early part of the twentieth century, the viaduct is about 240 metres long and nearly 40 metres high.* Bear left when the path forks, heading downhill. Soon after passing the tiny **Chapel-in-the-Wood**, you're back at river level again.

**3.** Nearing **Cotehele Quay**, take the path on the left. A few metres beyond the car park, bear left along the path signposted to the mill. (There are public toilets on

© Crown copyright and/or database right. All rights reserved. Licence number 100047867

Walk 10 – **Lishe Coffee Shop,** Calstock & Cotehele

**Calstock Viaduct mirrored in the Tamar**

the right here.) *Peaceful now, this would've been a busy spot in the nineteenth century, with cargo being loaded and unloaded and paddle steamers taking sightseers up the River Tamar.* After the **Discovery Centre**, bear left along the lane. After the bridge, go left at a T-junction — towards Bohetherick and St Dominick.

**4.** Soon after the road bends right, take the broad path climbing sharp right, part of the **St Dominica Trail**. Keep straight on at the next waymarker post, ignoring the path to the left and another to the right. Nearing the **woodland edge**, bear right at another waymarker, staying in the shade of the trees. As this trail swings down to the right, ignore a grassy route on the right, but then bear right along a narrower, but better used trail. At the next junction, immediately after crossing a **tiny stream**, turn right.

**5.** Turn right at the road and, in about 120 metres, turn left along the track leading to **Cotehele Mill**. *These buildings, once used to grind grain into flour, date from the nineteenth century, although there have probably been mills here for several centuries.* Take the next path on the right,

*The stunning Cotehele House and gardens*

passing some outbuildings on the right. Cross the **bridge** over **Morden Stream** and go sharp left at the next path junction. Bear left at an early fork.

**6.** Just before a **small bridge** at the **weir**, take the path climbing steeply right through **Elbow Wood**. Keep to the broader path as lesser trails go right and then left. At a T-junction, go right and quickly left. Turn left again at the next T-junction.

**7.** Cross the road and climb the steps opposite to continue through the trees, soon passing above **Cotehele Quay**. Turn left up a surfaced lane.

Ignore the turning for the disabled parking on the right but then turn right, following signs for the house and gardens. As the lane swings left in front of **Cotehele House**, go through the gap in the wall on the right. (You'll see the National Trust ticket office on the left, with The Barn café beyond.) Cross the gravel area to pick up a path to the right of the **toilet block**. You're soon able to sneak a peek at the house and gardens, after which the path swings down to the right, briefly overlapping with part of the earlier route. Bear left at a fork, climbing again. Joining a route from the left, the broad path contours the wooded hillside.

Walk 10 – **Lishe Coffee Shop,** Calstock & Cotehele

**8.** At the next junction, turn sharp right, descending steeply into **Danescombe Valley**. Keep right along a rough track at the bottom. Soon after the ruins of **Danescombe Sawmill**, you'll see the path to Cotehele House to the right again — at waypoint two. Keep left here, soon joining the outward lane to retrace your steps to the car park in **Calstock**. ♦

### Cotehele House

*The house at Cotehele was largely built in 1458 by Sir Richard Edgcumbe who fought alongside Henry Tudor at the Battle of Bosworth Field. Like the nearby mill and quay, it is managed by the National Trust and is open to the public. Interesting features include tapestries, armour, the turret clock and a mechanical prosthetic arm with moveable fingers that may have been used by a seventeenth-century soldier injured in battle.*

# Useful Information

### South Cornwall
The official tourism website for Cornwall covers everything from accommodation and places to eat to events and ideas for days out – **www.visitcornwall.com/places/south-cornwall**

### Cornwall Area of Outstanding Natural Beauty
The Cornwall AONB covers Bodmin Moor and several stretches of the South Cornwall coast, including the Lizard Peninsula – **www.cornwall-aonb.gov.uk**

### Selected Tourist Information Centres
**Visit Cornwall Information Service**, 30 Boscawen Street, Truro, TR1 2QQ; 01872 261735
**Welcome to West Cornwall Centre** (National Trust), Station Approach, Penzance, TR18 2NF; 01736 335530
**Fal River Visitor Information Centre**, 11 Market Strand, Falmouth, TR11 3DF; 01326 741194
**Launceston TIC,** Broad Street, Launceston, PL15 8AA; 01566 772321
**Liskeard TIC,** Foresters Hall, Pike Street, Liskeard, PL14 3JE; 01579 349148
**Looe TIC,** Looe Community Hub, The Millpool, West Looe, PL13 2AF; 01503 262255
**Lostwithiel TIC**, Community Centre, Pleyber Christ Way, Lostwithiel, PL22 0EH; 01208 872207
**The Roseland Visitor Centre**, The Millennium Rooms, The Square, St Mawes, TR2 5AG; 01326 270440

### Rail Travel
Cornwall's mainline stations include Liskeard, Bodmin Parkway, Lostwithiel, St Austell, Redruth, Truro and Penzance. There are also branch lines that serve the South Cornwall coast, terminating at Falmouth Docks and Looe.
National Rail Enquiries – **www.nationalrail.co.uk**; 03457 484950

### Bus Travel
For details of buses serving South Cornwall and to plan journeys, visit **www.travelinesw.com** or phone 0871 200 22 33 (telephone lines are staffed daily, 7am-8pm)

### Camping
Cornwall is a popular area for camping, with many sites owned by or affiliated to the Camping and Caravanning Club: 024 7647 5426 | **www.campingandcaravanningclub.co.uk**